W9-AMS-664

Discord

BURBANK MS LIBRARY 043

Discard

Choosing
a Career in
Information
Science

BURBANK MS LIBRARY 043

The amount of information available to us is often overwhelming, and not all of it is useful, so we rely on librarians to organize and disseminate it.

Choosing a Career in Information Science

Laura Leone

The Rosen Publishing Group, Inc.
New York

To Mom and Dad, who taught me to love books.

Published in 2002 by The Rosen Publishing Group, Inc.
29 East 21st Street, New York, NY 10010

Copyright © 2002 by The Rosen Publishing Group, Inc.

First Edition

All rights reserved. No part of this book may be reproduced in any form without permission in writing from the publisher, except by a reviewer.

Library of Congress Cataloging-in-Publication Data

Leone, Laura.
Choosing a career in information science / by Laura Leone. — 1st ed.
p. cm. — (World of work)
Includes bibliographical references (p.) and index.
ISBN 0-8239-3569-8 (lib. bdg.)
1. Library science—Vocational guidance—Juvenile literature.
2. Librarians—Juvenile literature. 3. Libraries—Juvenile literature. 4. Information science—Vocational guidance—Juvenile literature. [1. Library science—Vocational guidance. 2. Information science—Vocational guidance. 3. Librarians. 4. Libraries. 5. Vocational guidance.]
I. Title. II. World of work (New York, N.Y.)
Z665.5 .L46 2001
020'.23—dc21
                       2001002697

Manufactured in the United States of America

Contents

WꟼW

Introduction

*E*ileen Lundberg is a seventh grader at Fee Junior High. Last term she had to do an extra credit report on the American Civil War for her history class. Her school textbook had loads of information, but she needed to focus on a specific point in the war. Eileen went to her school librarian, who was able to help her narrow her topic and select materials for her project.

Janice O'Leary, a writer, decided to vacation in Japan last spring. Unsure about how to start planning her trip, she headed to her local library. There, the reference librarian assisted her in finding travel books on Japan, which helped Janice draw up her itinerary.

There are many people, like Eileen Lundberg and Janice O'Leary, who need information for their work and leisure. Our world today is filled with more types of information than ever before.

More information is available to people today than ever before. Librarians acquire and organize information and make it accessible to the public.

The amount of information can be overwhelming, and all of it is not always useful to us. Therefore, we need people who are trained to organize such information and make it available in a presentable way to us. Librarians are trained to do just this. They acquire information, organize it, make it accessible to the public, and recommend ways to use it.

Librarians are made up of all types of women and men, but they often have certain things in common: a love for books and knowledge, and a desire to share that love with other people. There are many ways a person can help others if he or she becomes a librarian. In this book, you will learn about reference librarians, the librarians who help you directly with your requests. You will also meet librarians who work more closely with books and other materials and less directly with the public.

There are also catalogers and technical processors. These are the people who work behind the scenes to acquire new materials and prepare them for public consumption by classifying them and giving them book covers, cards and pockets, and bar codes. We will see conservationists, who repair damaged, overused books. We will meet archivists who compile and organize materials that are no longer current, meaning they are no longer in daily use, but have some kind of historical or intellectual value that renders them worth keeping. Archivists first determine what materials these are, and then how to save them so they can be useful to current and future generations. The entire field of information science has been affected by the advent of the Internet; it has completely changed the way we think about information. Now there are jobs for cyberlibrarians, who deal specifically with information on the World Wide Web.

Librarians are able to work in diverse environments. The most common library work environments include public libraries (such as your town library), academic libraries (such as the local college library), privately endowed research libraries (such as a specific cultural center in a town), government libraries (such as the one in your city hall), school libraries, and special libraries (such as the French Library in Boston).

In a town such as New City, New York, for example, which has a population of approximately 40,000, there are librarians hard at work, not only in the town's New City Free Library but also in law firms; the elementary, middle, and high schools;

Librarians work in many different environments, such as public libraries, academic libraries, private research libraries, government libraries, school libraries, and special libraries.

businesses; private libraries; town government offices; city hall; and even the prison attached to city hall. As you can see, there is a wide variety of settings in which a library professional can work, depending on his or her interests and credentials.

According to the U.S. National Center for Education Statistics and the *Bowker Annual Library and Book Trade Almanac*, there are an estimated 60,000 library professionals working in public libraries and 45,000 library professionals working in academic libraries (postsecondary level) in the United States today. There are up to 4,000 library professionals working in America's three national libraries: the Library of Congress (in Washington, D.C.), the National Library of Medicine (in Bethesda, Maryland), and the National Agricultural Library (in Beltsville, Maryland). The U.S. National Commission on Libraries and Information Science (NCLIS) tracks statistics such as these. According to its Web site, the NCLIS "serves as a liaison [go-between] to the library community, organizes meetings and training workshops, organizes training and technical assistance, monitors trends, and advises NCES [National Center for Education Statistics] on policy matters." A recent study done by the NCLIS measured public libraries and use of the Internet in 2000, for example.

All library professionals work together toward a main goal: making the information found in books, documents, and audio and visual materials available and useful to whoever needs them for whatever reason. In general, librarians are people who love reading and what books have to offer, and who want to share this enthusiasm with others. As they help others, librarians are always learning.

What Does a Librarian Do?

Traditionally, as in fields like teaching and midwifery, most librarians have been women. That has changed today, as women regularly work in previously male-dominated fields and vice versa. There are still more women than men in the field, but librarians have come a long way from the stereotype of the woman with a hair bun who tells people to keep quiet! Librarians are hard workers who love books and like sharing knowledge with others. They want to help people discover new things by reading.

At Your Service

In an age of information and technology, librarians play a crucial role in helping to organize and disseminate knowledge. There are different types of librarians who oversee the book process before a patron of a library gets to use it. First, acquisitions librarians get to choose which books are appropriate for their particular collections. Depending on the type of library, books are usually donated or

11

BURBANK MS LIBRARY 043

purchased. Once a book is acquired, it needs to be processed by a cataloger. Catalogers assign a call number, make up book pockets and cards, and give the book a dust jacket for protection. A card for the catalog must be generated, and in most cases, with the exception of smaller libraries, an electronic record is created. Then the book can go out to the circulation staff, where it will be put into the open collection. This means that the book is available for a reference librarian to locate or for a patron to check out. Librarians are involved at every point in the process.

To understand how and where librarians work, let's look for a moment at a typical school day in the life of a college student named Thomas. Thomas goes to his university's library to drop off a book he checked out last week. Here, he encounters circulation clerks, the librarians who monitor the movement of books in and out of the library. When Thomas drops off his book, the circulation clerks use a database to check it back into the collection. Then Thomas is ready to do research for a term paper he has to write.

While on his way to see a reference librarian, he notices cases along the wall, filled with papers and old books. Thomas stops for a moment to view them. The cases hold eighteenth-century letters and books written by a local playwright. Thomas sees a sign that reads, "Visit the University Archives, Fifth Floor." Intrigued, he makes a note to himself to investigate the fifth floor. Next, Thomas walks to the reference desk, where three librarians are sorting through texts and papers. He asks one of them to help him find

Each of the thousands of books acquired by a library must be processed by a cataloger, who assigns a call number, makes up pockets and cards, and gives the book a dust jacket.

information on a particular place in Spain, the subject of his history paper. The reference librarian walks Thomas to a particular section of the library, where history books on Spain are kept. They then approach a computer terminal and the librarian explains the various online databases available to him for research. Finally, the librarian suggests that Thomas search for old newspaper articles in the serials department. On his way there, Thomas passes a sign for the cataloging department, as well as for the interlibrary loan area, where people can request books held by other libraries. Once in the serials department, a serials librarian helps him find the appropriate papers and magazines.

Remembering the sign he saw when he first entered the library, Thomas takes the stairs to the fifth floor. Immediately, he sees cases full of materials, artwork, and papers. It is a busy place, and staff members are walking around, talking, and working. One person is emptying a case of items from a past exhibition. A man who says he is the head archivist at the university archives asks if Thomas needs any help. Thomas looks around and sees a variety of materials on display, such as old cameras, magazine articles, photographs, and a collection of rare maps. All of it looks interesting, as if a story is being told.

All of these library professionals are needed to work in one academic library. Some stay behind the scenes, and others are up front, ready to assist Thomas and other students directly with their research. In any given library, archives, and even some workplaces, library professionals are hard at

Librarians who work for businesses make more money than those who work for public libraries. Businesses usually have more money to buy books and other resources.

work organizing, interpreting, and preparing books and other forms of knowledge so that they are accessible to college students, researchers, and anyone with information requests.

Salaries

As in any job field, librarians at different levels of education and experience command a range of levels of compensation. Librarians who work for corporations, such as law firms or businesses, make more money than those who work for public or school libraries. Corporations usually have more money at their disposal to allocate, or distribute, toward salaries. They also often have more funds to channel toward resources for their libraries. A typical salary range for a corporate librarian or corporate archivist is $40,000 to $60,000 per year.

Over the years, federal and state governments have cut funding to school and public libraries throughout the United States. As a result, many libraries are chronically short of funds for resources, creating frustration for librarians.

Librarians who work for the government at the federal, state, or provincial level may get higher salaries than those working at the city or town level, since the government may not have the particular financial constraints that cities or towns may encounter. This would depend on the city's or town's own budget. However, government positions may have monetary restrictions of their own, depending on the current political administration; some presidents channel more money toward education and libraries than others. Salaries for government librarians range from $35,000 to $70,000 per year.

School and public librarians' salaries are determined by the budget of the particular school or library and the district in which the school operates. It is often the case that libraries are short of funds for resources, and librarians encounter frustrations due to this. School and public librarians can make anywhere from $23,000 to $40,000 a year.

Privately funded libraries and special collections libraries often have more money at their disposal, as a result of grants and endowments. Therefore, librarians in these jobs may make more money than others, often in the range of $35,000 to $80,000 per year. Certain positions in the academic world pay more, and university librarians likely command higher salaries than smaller college librarians; though, if a small college has a significant amount of money from donations, for example, there may be more money for the library and for staff salaries.

Librarians who work as archivists often deal with valuable historical records and documents, although, like other librarians, they also encounter budget frustrations.

Museum work for archivists and librarians has a similar pay scale. Historical societies and town museums generally have smaller budgets than state and federal institutions, such as a city's museum of fine arts. Therefore, an archivist working at your town's historical society will make anywhere from $23,000 to $35,000 a year. An archivist at a large city museum may make $32,000 to $45,000 a year. As in any field, specialists often garner higher salaries because of their specific expertise. So, a museum may be willing to pay more for a nineteenth-century photographs archivist if its collections hold many photographs from that time period.

Salaries depend on the way individual organizations choose to allocate their monetary funds. Some places dedicate money to technology and not salaries. It is important to realize that management positions pay more, and job salaries are always dependent upon experience and individual credentials. Note that the field of library science is not known for its high salaries! People who are motivated by material gains are generally not found in library positions. Keep in mind, however, that there are always opportunities for advancement, and one can receive ample rewards, both monetary and intellectual, in the diverse settings that are available to librarians.

Librarians share knowledge not only with their patrons but also with each other. Organizations exist in which librarians can keep each other informed about new techniques and issues in the field. Often these organizations are specific to particular types of library work. To contact these organizations, please check the For More Information section at the back of this book.

There is no certification that is needed to work in library sciences. Most librarians do go on from their undergraduate education to get a master of science in library science degree (this is explained in chapter 3). The master of library science degree enables a librarian to understand more about information and how it is organized. Once librarians have specialized, they will go on to conferences, seminars, and organization meetings to further their education.

Ask Yourself

Do I enjoy helping people? Do I love books and other forms of information? Do I like to learn as much as I can? Do many different subjects interest me?

History of Libraries and Information Science

In ancient times, the Greeks and Romans emphasized learning, and our own educational systems have been greatly influenced by their ideas. Alexandria, Egypt, was the center of all learning during the time of Alexander the Great, from around 300 BC to the end of that millennium. The city hosted two renowned royal libraries and a museum, where questions about science, literature, and history could be researched. The predecessor to modern-day libraries began in Alexandria, and the whole idea of libraries as places of reference and learning was established and enhanced. At the time, all books were handwritten on scrolls of animal skins or on paper made from plants. The libraries in Alexandria held hundreds of thousands of scrolls filled with information, and the librarians in Alexandria helped users sort through the materials, just like librarians today. They were also responsible for keeping the scrolls organized and in order. One head librarian was renowned astronomer and scholar Eratosthenes, who not

The libraries in Alexandria, Egypt, named for Alexander the Great *(above)*, were the centers of knowledge during that time and the predecessors to modern libraries.

only assisted others in their own research, but also pursued his own interests in astronomy while he worked there.

As time went on, the concept of libraries evolved, depending on what was happening in different parts of the world. For a long time, only upper-class men, government leaders, university professors, and clergymen knew how to read. In most of fifteenth-century Europe, for instance, women were denied access to libraries because it was decided that they did not need to know how to read to perform their daily tasks. The idea of reading for personal enrichment was considered appropriate only for men. People knew of the world only what they heard or saw in their own towns or villages.

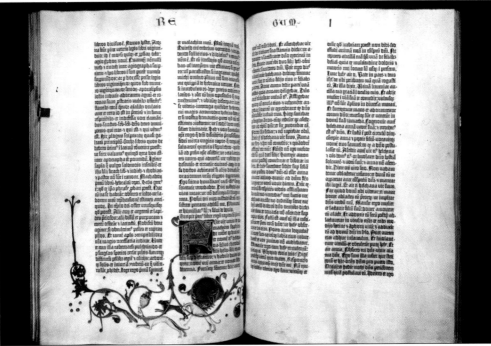

By using metal letters to make impressions on paper, Johannes Gutenberg developed movable type, which enabled the mass production of books. In 1454, he began printing the so-called Gutenberg Bible, which is still renowned today for its beauty.

Most texts were written in Latin, which was the language of the church at the time, and the church was the dominant power. Therefore, members of the clergy were often the only ones in certain parts of the world who knew how to read. Monks were often responsible for transcribing different texts and often hand-lettered the books. It is thanks to their meticulous efforts that we have retained many of these old texts today in museums and libraries all over the world.

In the fifteenth century, a process was invented that changed not only the way people looked at books but the whole concept of information. In the 1430s, German Johannes Gutenberg conceived the idea of movable type. By using small metal letters to make impressions on paper, one could duplicate books. No one had ever accomplished this before. The first copies Gutenberg made were of a well-known grammar book, since grammar was considered the basis of learning at the time. Because they were used to the handwritten manuscripts and preferred to read from them, people were slow to catch on to the idea of printed books. Eventually, scholars and other professionals started to see the advantages of making books available to more people.

In 1454, Gutenberg started work on his greatest achievement: the Gutenberg Bible, known today for its precision and beauty. He made 200 copies and also printed a Latin dictionary and encyclopedia and an astronomical calendar. The concept spread quickly after that, and by 1500, there were 1,000 printers across Europe. Books became more available because they could be reproduced, and this allowed ordinary people access to knowledge. Some believe that this development signaled the end of the Middle Ages.

Organizing Information

Once information was readily available and books became more commonplace, librarians had to decide how to organize them so users could find what they needed quickly. Depending on the size of a collection, materials can be organized in many ways. A classification system is a way of coding books, giving each a special identification number that is particular to that one book. This enables a user to find the book. Factors used when coming up with a classification number (usually called a book's "call number") include author, title, subject, and year published.

There are several major classification systems that are used worldwide. In America, the two most popular are the Library of Congress system and the Dewey decimal system. Overseas in Europe and other parts of the world, a system called the Universal decimal classification system is used, and this is similar to the Dewey decimal system. All systems use letters and numbers to assign books their own special call number, and these numbers decide where in a library the book will be located. Therefore, users have an easier time finding books because books with the same subjects or authors are often shelved together.

National Libraries

In addition to public and private libraries, most countries have national libraries. A national library is a place that keeps the holdings of a country safe. It keeps track of books copyrighted and published in the country. National libraries are often visited by researchers who need information on items in the collection and are often located in the nation's capital, with branches in other parts of the country.

In the United States, the Library of Congress can be found in Washington, D.C., and holds 119 million items, according to its Web site. It is the largest library in the world, receiving an average of 22,000 new items every day! Not only does it hold books copyrighted in United States, but it also contains many materials published in other countries.

The Library of Congress in Washington, D.C., is the largest library in the world, with more than 119 million holdings. It receives some 22,000 new submissions each day.

Founded in 1800 with an initial donation from Thomas Jefferson, the Library of Congress is also the oldest federal institution in the nation. The National Library of Canada, located in Toronto, serves a similar function for Canada. It seeks to preserve Canada's cultural heritage so that it is available for future generations. Overseas, the British Library, holder of the Gutenberg Bible, has collections spanning 3,000 years of history, with items from every continent. Like most national libraries, the British Library has exhibitions, workshops, and works of art for the public to appreciate. Many national libraries like the Library of Congress also have offices overseas, and these serve to look out for new acquisitions and represent the country's interests abroad.

Now, in the twenty-first century, the Internet is in full force, and most libraries, museums, and archives have an online presence in addition to their physical presence. The national libraries mentioned in this book all have extensive Web sites. The Library of Congress is at http://www.loc.gov, the National Library of Canada's Web site is http://www.nlc-bnc.ca, and the British Library has collections online at http://www.bl.uk. These Web sites can be excellent resources on their own, and they also allow researchers to investigate the library's holdings to see if a trip there is worthwhile. The most important thing to realize is that many of these libraries are open to everyone and anyone who wants more information on specific topics, or people who just want to see materials for their own personal enrichment. Access to knowledge is the key phrase, and knowledge lets people understand and appreciate their own history.

Ask Yourself

Am I interested in the history of books? Have I ever thought about how books are printed and published? Would I like to visit my own national library to see what books and exhibits they have there?

Becoming a Librarian

If you love reading books and researching information, working in the library sciences could be for you. You can go to your librarian at school and ask him or her about the job and what a typical workday is like. Think about times when your school librarian has helped you. Were there times when you got stuck on your own and had to enlist the help of the librarian to help you understand how to find a book, or even where to begin?

Many librarians do not end up studying library science in a formal setting until the graduate school level of education. You'll find that librarians have educational backgrounds in anything from English literature to business. Many archivists have backgrounds in history. There aren't any formal library science programs at the undergraduate (college) level, although in the last few years, some colleges have developed coursework in their undergraduate curriculum to include information science subject courses. For instance, New Mexico State University has an information literacy course listed in their undergraduate course catalog.

There are many programs at the graduate level, however, and this is where most library science professionals begin to study information science, working toward a master of science in library sciences, commonly known as an M.L.S. There are some fifty schools of library and information science in the United States, United Kingdom, and Canada; one can also find dual degree programs in history and library science, offered by Simmons College in Boston, or library science and business at Kent State University in Ohio, for example. Dalhousie University in Halifax, Nova Scotia, and the University of Toronto have well-known programs in Canada.

One of the main things students of information science learn is how to organize information. Students learn new ways to consider organizing ideas and concepts. They learn about organizing subjects using classification systems, such as the Library of Congress system or the Dewey decimal system.

A librarian might advise someone who is interested in information science to seek a broad liberal arts education. Knowledge in many diverse areas is important. A student should study subjects in which he or she is interested, but one should try to take classes on a variety of topics, from literature and history to psychology and sociology. In a library science program, a student will learn all the necessary skills to become an excellent librarian. There, the student will learn about the vast types of reference materials available, such as dictionaries and encyclopedias. Library students also learn Web skills, how to classify and catalog books, and methods of book preservation. Elective classes on

If you are interested in becoming a librarian, it helps to familiarize yourself with a variety of subjects. In a library science program, you will learn about reference materials, research skills, how to classify and catalog books, and how to preserve old books.

public school media, archives, literacy, international librarianship, and book repair are also offered, to name just a few. This allows a future librarian to specialize and decide what kind of work he or she wants to do.

Library science programs are usually filled with coursework and internships. Unless a library student has a particular career in mind, such as school media library specialist or archivist, he or she is encouraged to explore a variety of course offerings in the program in order to be exposed to the many career choices available. Reference librarians, for instance, take the same core library courses as archivists. However, archives students are also required to take extra courses specific to archives. Conservationists will take the same core courses as well. In the majority of graduate programs these core courses include reference, cataloging, and research and management. However, many conservationists will go on to smaller workshops and programs once their library science degrees are finished to do particular work in the conservation field. For example, those who want to work in school libraries may take a course on literature for adolescents, which archivist or reference students would not take. Catalogers may take advanced cataloging courses that deal specifically with types of books, such as rare books or manuscripts. Archivists can take courses in museum exhibition work or manuscript appraisal.

Flexibility Is Key

Your interests may change over the course of your educational experience. Sara Peterson entered her library program intent on becoming an archivist. However, when she took the cataloging course, she was pleasantly surprised at how much she enjoyed it, and therefore pursued a part-time job in a cataloging department at a private library while still in school. Her interest in archives had not waned, and she was also able to obtain experience working in an archives through an internship at a local historical center. When Sara was near to completion of the program, she knew that she wanted to pursue a job that combined her archives and cataloging skills. Experience and skills in two different areas of the library profession worked to her benefit because she had more to offer a potential employer. Sara now works in a museum setting, where she catalogs archival manuscripts, thus combining the two areas of library science she enjoys most.

What You'll Learn

Each class has different challenges for the student. One typical archives class is called preservation, where students learn about the care and repair of books and other archival materials, such as manuscripts (works on paper that have not been bound into book form), objects (such as diaries), and photographs. Courses are often taught by guest lecturers as well as by professors. The Northeast Document Conservation Center (NEDCC) in Andover, Massachusetts, often sends conservation specialists to library schools to teach students not only how to repair damaged books but also preventative measures so that books won't get to the repair stage in the first place. Students can see how books are sewn together by hand or glued together by machine. They learn about disaster planning and how to maintain collections in different environments. For example, have you ever thought about the problems a library in Bermuda might have due to its hot, humid climate? (The ideal environment for book storage, for example, is about $75°$ Fahrenheit, at a humidity level of 65 percent.) Or what about libraries in countries that are prone to natural disasters like earthquakes and hurricanes?

In a photographic archives class, students learn about the different types of photographic processes and how to manage and care for photographic collections. Wearing special gloves, students are allowed to handle a variety of photographs, and they are asked to identify the various types of photos, such as tintypes and daguerreotypes (both nineteenth-century processes), and gelatin silver prints.

To effectively catalog and store photographic archives, library students may learn about types of photographic processes and how to manage and care for photographic collections. They learn how to identify many kinds of photos, such as tintypes, daguerreotypes, and gelatin silver prints.

On the library side, reference classes teach students how to research print and electronic resources, such as encyclopedias, Web sites, and databases. This way, when people come into libraries looking for particular information, librarians will know exactly what sources to use to find it.

The management class takes a different approach. It is essentially business management, focusing on managing budgets, staff, and collections. Students read and analyze case studies about libraries and other businesses, in the hopes that they will one day be able to apply this knowledge to real-life situations. One common theme in all these classes is hands-on experience. Whether a student visits work environments or just handles different library and archives materials in class, he or she can get a feel for what working in the field will be like.

There is generally no thesis to be completed at the end of the library science program, but a student has the option to continue his or her education to obtain a doctorate in a specialized subject. Many librarians who have doctorates go on to teach in library programs. Internships allow students to experience work in different settings firsthand. Most courses require students to work a certain number of hours in a particular workplace, such as a university library or state archives. The hours students work in these places help fulfill the requirements of the M.L.S.

Librarians often help people who are searching for information, so it helps to have strong interpersonal skills if you want to pursue this career.

Sara Peterson's coursework in cataloging led her to pursue direct work experience in a cataloging department. In the case of Monica Higgins, an internship experience determined the course of her study. Monica entered her library science program unsure of what she wanted to study. After taking an archives course called Archives for Nonarchives Students, for which an internship was required, she decided that she wanted to become an archivist. Her internship, assigned by the teacher, was at the archives of a small town's historical society. Here she helped the archivist on staff (small-town archives often employ only one archivist) research historical houses in the area. Many visitors to the society wanted to know more about the history of their homes. Monica was able to confer with town records, old photographs, land deeds, and other manuscripts in the society's collection and provide the visitors with exact information about when their houses were built, previous owners, and other historical information of interest. As a result of this positive experience, Monica registered for more archives classes in her subsequent terms.

Internships such as these can be very rewarding for students, since they can learn about the field and also can make contacts for future reference and job possibilities.

Ask Yourself

If you think you might enjoy working as a librarian, ask yourself some relevant questions: Do I enjoy school? Am I excited by the prospect of learning new things? Would I be interested in learning about how dictionaries and encyclopedias are created? What areas of library science are most intriguing to me?

Working in the Field

As you have read, there are many different types of librarians who work in a variety of environments. Depending on your interests and the type of setting in which you prefer to spend your time, you can choose to work with the public or more intimately with books, in a library or for a large corporation. Aside from the same general love of books and the desire to provide information to others, librarians have different interests and personalities. They are part of a larger community dedicated to sharing knowledge.

Reference Librarian

The librarians with whom most of us are familiar are those who help us when we ask questions at the library: reference librarians. Reference librarians also field questions from people who phone the library and need information quickly. As e-mail has become more popular, many reference librarians find themselves with an inbox of questions as well. Reference librarians are often responsible for making sure the reference sources are up to date.

Reference librarians answer questions from those who e-mail, phone, or come into the library. To ensure they are always available to anyone who needs them, reference materials may not be taken out of the library.

The reference materials in any library cannot be taken out of the library—that way they are always available to anyone who needs them.

Melanie Schneider works as a reference librarian at a private library. Each day, she has multiple tasks that include her own work as well as helping others with their research. A typical day for her involves sorting through e-mail reference inquiries and investigating questions using the vast online and print resources in her library. She also is likely to field questions from patrons who phone the reference desk. Some people need information quickly, but other requests involve more of Melanie's time. In that case, Melanie will comb the online database for books relevant to the topic and then call the patron back with her findings. She also helps people use the online catalog on the library's Web site. Since the library has five floors and many different collections, there are times when she has to show reference patrons around the library and point them in the right direction so they can find the books they need. One of the most enjoyable parts of the job, according to Melanie, is talking with patrons about their interests and research. For example, she helped a writer who was writing a novel set in nineteenth-century San Francisco find information on that time and place.

Cataloger

Catalogers have different experiences than reference librarians because they usually don't deal directly with the patrons. They work behind the scenes

Catalogers work behind the scenes to organize the books a library acquires. They determine where each book belongs in the collection.

and are the ones who see the books as the library acquires them. Catalogers get to handle the books, pore over the subjects, and determine where any given book belongs in the collection.

William Evans is a cataloger at a public library in a big city. His workday consists of examining the latest books to make it into the collection. He is also on the new books recommendation committee, so he spends part of his day reading trade journals like *American Libraries* and *Kirkus Review* to keep abreast of the latest books published in many areas of interest. William also searches a large national database for information about books in the collection. He uses Library of Congress subject heading books to assign each book a call number, and then he types up a book card and pocket for each. He loves working closely with the books themselves.

Conservationist

What happens when a book is overused and falling apart? It is important to keep library books in proper condition so they can be used again and again. Conservationists are specialist librarians who assess damaged books and repair them. Not all libraries have conservation departments. Sometimes, a library will send books out to another place to be repaired on an ad hoc (as needed) basis. Conservation departments often find themselves busy with a significant number of damaged books. It is their job to make sure the books are in good enough shape to go back into the open collection where they will continue to be used by patrons.

Archivist

Archivists work with slightly different materials than regular librarians. Most archivists go to library school like librarians, but many have backgrounds in history and have special education particular to the subject of the collections in which they are working. Archivists are liable to work with books, manuscripts, film and audio materials, and other objects, such as war medals, diaries, and journals. They also work with other items, called ephemera, like theater playbills and print advertisements, that were by-products of daily life during their use. The items will vary, depending on the collection on which the archivist is working.

An archivist may work with many different information storage systems, such as magnetic tape, as seen here. Magnetic tape vaults can store huge collections of data, and the archivist must know how to access them.

Lisa Starzyk-Weldon is an archivist for a mid-sized urban library. One of her main projects is to create finding aids for the collections in her library's archives. Finding aids are like manuals that provide users with information on each particular collection. They are significant because the items in every individual collection are arranged differently, according to the type of collection and the way the archivist has chosen to organize them.

When a collection is acquired by an archive, the first thing the archivist will ask himself or herself is, "What is the most efficient way these items can be arranged so a researcher will have the quickest access to them?" Archivists create finding aids to tell prospective researchers how the collection has been arranged, and this facilitates their work. Lisa Starzyk-Weldon posts many of her finding aids on the library's Web site, so people from other states and countries who need to know exactly what materials her library owns can investigate before they travel to the library to see the collections themselves.

As we will see in the next chapter, there are many other types of librarians and archivists. School librarians specialize in school curriculum, and teachers often turn to them for advice on resources. Museums employ archivists to assist in curating exhibitions. Corporate librarians and archivists work in companies and businesses to help arrange and maintain the records of these organizations. Law firms often employ teams of librarians to support the lawyers with their case research.

School librarians specialize in the curriculum that the school is required by law to teach its students. Teachers often rely on them for advice about resources.

A Supportive Community

The library world is one large community of individuals who share resources and advice. Many organizations exist as forums for librarians, archivists, catalogers, rare-book librarians, and other types of information professionals. For instance, the Society of American Archivists, based in Chicago, has over 3,400 members, according to its Web site (http://www.archivists.org). It addresses issues specific to the archival field through its quarterly journal, *American Archivist*. The American Library Association has a journal called *American Libraries*, and its Web site (http://www.ala.org) presents the encouragement of such issues as diversity and literacy as their goals.

Electronic list-serves enable people working in libraries all over the world to assist one another with problems regarding information research and accessibility.

The Canadian Library Association, based in Ottawa, represents the interests of libraries in Canada. According to the organization's Web site (http://www.cla.ca), the CLA is advised by over thirty interest groups and committees. Other organizations cater to more specific aspects of the field, such as the Public Library Association and the Association for Library Service to Children. They host conferences, offer professional education, and give recognition to leaders in the library community. There are also electronic list-serves, where people working in libraries all over the world can assist each other with everyday problems and concerns.

One of the things libraries pride themselves on is their accessibility to all people. Most libraries are accessible to the handicapped, and many offer resources specifically for disabled patrons. The

Andrew Heiskell Library for the Blind and Physically Handicapped is a library in New York City that is equipped with specially formatted materials, such as talking books, books in Braille, and a machine that converts text into speech. The children's room at this library has puzzles, globes, and other objects that help visually impaired children identify shapes. The library is part of a national network designed to cater to people with physical handicaps.

Ask Yourself

Do I like helping others with their work, or would I be more comfortable working more closely with books? Does the thought of working with objects, manuscripts, journals, or rare books interest me? Where do I think I would like to work? How have librarians in my life affected me? Have I thought about working as a clerk at my own town library?

A Career with Many Options

Like the average person, librarians often have a diverse number of interests. One of the fun things about working in library science is that it gives a prospective librarian or archivist many choices about where to work. Public and school libraries always need many types of librarians, such as catalogers and reference librarians. But, as you've learned, large corporations employ librarians and archivists as well. Law firms need librarians on staff to research court cases. The Coca-Cola Company, for example, needs librarians and archivists to maintain the historical records of the organization. Museums need archivists to help set up exhibitions.

The academic world offers many jobs. Universities need librarians and archivists for the acquisition, organization, and maintenance of what can be vast collections. Large universities may have several libraries on their campuses, including those devoted to specific subjects. Harvard University, for example, supports Baker Library, which is a business library, and Yenching Library, which is devoted to East Asian materials. Often, librarians need to know the language of the country from which materials in their collections came.

Peg Fulton, administrative librarian of the Loeb Classical Library at Harvard University Press, stands by Latin and Greek texts that have been published in English. The library is updating and modernizing the translations.

Curating

An important aspect of the library field involves the spread of information. People worldwide need the expertise of others to further their own research and knowledge. In addition to the librarians we see every day in town and school libraries, we learn as much from librarians and archivists in other settings, even though we may not deal directly with them. For example, the Montreal Museum of Fine Arts has displayed an exhibit called Hitchcock and Art, from which visitors learn about Alfred Hitchcock's films, his influences, and his private collection of movies. To create an exhibit like this, a team of archivists first had to see what was in the museum's own collection that could be used. Then inquiries were made to other museums, both national and international, regarding their collections. Museums often borrow works of art from other institutions and private collectors when they are setting up exhibits.

Since the Hitchcock exhibit explores the way art themes run through the film works of Alfred Hitchcock, several types of media are involved. Therefore, archivists who specialize in film media are the ones who put together the exhibit. Putting together an exhibit is called curating, and the people who do this are called curators. The two curators of the Hitchcock exhibit have different backgrounds: One is the current director of the Montreal Museum of Fine Arts, and the other is the director of the Cinémathèque Française in Paris. Both have an education in archives work, but one has more experience in general museum work. The other has worked specifically in film-oriented environments. The combination of their expertise gives the exhibit many layers, which allows for a stronger experience. Part of the enjoyment of archives work is getting to work with diverse types of materials, like film, art, letters, and objects. The added bonus of working side by side with colleagues with whom one can share experience and knowledge is also significant.

Assisting a Variety of People

Librarians often work with many different types of people in a variety of industries. Researchers in business, academics, and history, for example, all utilize the services of librarians for their work. One growing field is the field of genealogy—it is increasingly popular to create a family tree. Many people interested in genealogy have to go to their state archives or local libraries to do research on their ancestors. The Massachusetts State Archives branch in Boston has a special area set up just for people researching their family histories. It has materials such as passenger lists for boats that came into Boston, deeds lists, and birth and death certificates on file. The librarians and archivists who work at the archives assist people with the task of compiling the information that will be most useful to them. The advent of new technologies, such as the Internet and World Wide Web, has brought librarians together with Web specialists who want to develop certain types of content on

The Internet has revolutionized the ways information is organized, stored, and disseminated. It is safe to say, however, that computers will not replace books as providers of information in the near future.

their particular Web sites. Lawyers, doctors, and other professionals need to work with librarians to obtain information that is vital to them, but these professionals can also help librarians. For example, if a person comes to the library with a question about medicine, a librarian may need to investigate beyond the scope of the books in the library. He or she may have to call a medical professional in the area and acquire information on behalf of his or her patron. Librarians actively learn every day they are on the job, which can be very fulfilling. Librarians and archivists often find themselves acting as liaisons between researchers and other professionals who might have the information the researcher needs.

The End of Information Science?

When the World Wide Web became used more publicly, concerns were raised about the future of the printed book. How long would it last? As any archivist or conservationist will tell you, paper is still the longest-lasting material. We still have the Gutenberg Bible from the fifteenth century, while an electronic floppy disk will last only an average of eighty years. Many people still prefer to curl up with a good book rather than sit at the computer and read an e-book (electronic book). While the Web houses an incredible amount of information on its virtual pages, it is important to realize that the amount of material on any given topic still pales in comparison to what exists in printed books.

The Internet has increased the quantity of information available, so librarians are needed more than ever. They must learn Web skills in library science programs and be able to help patrons with searches and Web site navigation.

The Web can be a terrific resource, and it is vital in getting information to people who might not otherwise be able to get it. In many ways, it has made librarians' jobs easier, but it has not made the job of the librarian obsolete! If anything, the Internet has increased the amount of available information, and therefore more librarians are needed than ever before. Today, librarians learn Web skills in library science programs, and are equipped to help patrons with search-engine searches and Web site navigation. Since most museums, corporations, libraries, archives, and universities have Web sites, librarians are needed to help organize and develop content for these sites.

There is no sign that the existence and popularity of the Web will diminish the role of the librarian or make the printed book disappear. One important way librarians are striving to make the Web work for them is to get more information out there to more people. Let's say you want to use the collections of a certain library, but it is far away from your home, in another state or even another country. Since many libraries and archives now have items from their collections online, you can still access this information without ever leaving home.

The Library of Congress is a prime example of a library using the Web to make its collections more accessible to the general public. It has created the American Memory Project (found online at http://memory.loc.gov), described as "American history in words, sounds and pictures." It has taken multimedia, digitized documents, photographs, recorded sound, moving pictures, and text from the

Scott Price is a collector of rare and valuable historical books. He donated a multivolume book collection about slavery in America to the Kansas State University Library.

Library's Americana collections and put them online in a large searchable database for people worldwide to use. The project is a work in progress, and the LOC is adding items all the time. As of June 2001, there were seven million historical items included online.

The field of information science has not diminished over the last decade. If anything, more jobs have been created as a result of the vast amount of new electronic information produced by the Web. Enrollment in library science programs has remained steady, and more programs are being created, particularly ones with specific areas of study in mind. For instance, rare-book schools and conservation schools have gained more popularity for the continuing education of librarians. Organizations that employed librarians solely for print works now need librarians to handle all of the electronic resources available. Jobs for cyberlibrarians are now prevalent, since most institutions need Web sites, and therefore require librarians with Web skills to organize the content on these sites. People may think that the reliance on paper materials has decreased, leading to fewer jobs for librarians, but this is hardly the case. The use of books and other print materials has not lessened at all; resources such as the Web, DVDs, and CD-ROMs have only added to the responsibilities of librarians. The outlook for librarians in the twenty-first century is very encouraging and positive. With all the information we generate, who would organize and interpret it if we didn't have librarians? The job of a librarian as a liaison to knowledge is not likely to disappear anytime soon.

Glossary

acquisition librarian   Librarian who selects, orders, purchases, and receives new materials for a library collection.

archives   Organized collection of noncurrent records, preserved for their historical value.

archivist   Person, usually a librarian, who manages and maintains an archival collection.

call number   Code displayed on the label of each item in a library collection, which uniquely identifies it and gives its location on the shelf.

cataloger   Librarian primarily responsible for arranging books, periodicals, maps, and other materials of a specific collection in order.

circulation   Process of checking books and other materials in and out of a library.

classification system   Method of organizing library materials using specific coding to make them accessible to the public.

conservationist   Specially trained librarian who uses chemical or physical methods to preserve manuscripts, books, and other documents.

curator   Person in charge of creating and overseeing an exhibit or special collection.

cyberlibrarian   Librarian who researches and retrieves information using the Internet and other electronic resources.

daguerreotype   Nineteenth-century type of photograph produced on a silver plate.

ephemera   Collectibles; articles and items from a particular time or place.

Gutenberg Bible   Earliest known book to have been produced from movable type, probably printed between 1450 and 1455, in Mainz, Germany, by Johannes Gutenberg.

historical society   Nonprofit organization devoted to preserving the historical record of a place, person, or event.

holdings   Library collection.

manuscript   Book written entirely by hand, or a book in its prepublished state.

national library   Library funded by a national government to serve as a collection of all published and some unpublished materials of the nation.

processing   Everything done to a book after it is acquired by a library and before it is placed on the shelf, including cataloging, stamping, labeling, numbering, and putting on the jacketing.

reference librarian   Librarian who helps patrons find answers to their research questions.

special collection   Separate section in a library for rare books, manuscripts, personal papers, and other items that are not part of the regular collection.

For More Information

International Federation of Library Associations
    and Institutions
P.O. Box 95312
2509 CH The Hague
Netherlands
+31 70 3140884
Web site: http://www.ifla.org/index.htm

In the United States

American Library Association
50 East Huron
Chicago, IL 60611
(800) 545-2433
Web site: http://www.ala.org

Institute of Museum and Library Services
1100 Pennsylvania Avenue NW
Washington, DC 20506
(202) 606-8536
Web site: http://www.imls.gov

Library of Congress
101 Independence Avenue SE
Washington, DC 20540
(202) 707-5000
Web site: http://www.loc.gov

National Archives and Records Administration
700 Pennsylvania Avenue NW
Washington, DC 20408
(800) 234-8861
Web site: http://www.nara.gov

Society of American Archivists
527 South Wells Street, 5th Floor
Chicago, IL 60607-3922
(312) 922-0140
Web site: http://www.archivists.org

U.S. National Commission on Libraries and
    Information Science
1110 Vermont Avenue NW, Suite 820
Washington, DC 20005-3552
(202) 606-9200
Web site: http://www.nclis.gov

In Canada

Canadian Library Association
328 Frank Street
Ottawa, ON K2P 0X8
(613) 232-9625
Web site: http://www.cla.ca

National Library of Canada
395 Wellington Street
Ottawa, ON K1A 0N4
(877) 896-9481
Web site: http://www.nlc-bnc.ca

For Further Reading

Dickson, Paul. *The Library in America: A Celebration in Words and Pictures.* New York: Facts on File Publications, 1986.

Goodrum, Charles A. *Treasures of the Library of Congress.* New York: Harry N. Abrams Publishers, 1991.

Lord, Caroline M. *Diary of a Village Library.* Somersworth, NH: New Hampshire Publishing Company, 1971.

Kapr, Albert. *Johann Gutenberg: The Man and His Invention.* Translated by Douglas Martin. Brookfield, VT: Scolar Press, 1996.

Wedgeworth, Robert, ed. *ALA World Encyclopedia of Library and Information Services.* 3rd ed. Chicago, IL: American Library Association, 1993.

Index

A
acquisitions, 8, 11, 25, 39, 46
American Library
    Association, 43
American Memory Project,
    53–54
archivists/archives, 8, 12,
    14, 18, 26, 27, 29,
    30, 31, 33, 34–35,
    40–42, 43, 46, 48,
    49, 51, 53
Association for Library
    Services to Children, 44

B
book preservation, 29, 31
British Library, 25, 26

C
call numbers, 12, 23, 24, 39
Canadian Library
    Association, 44
catalogers/cataloging, 8,
    12, 14, 30, 34, 38–39,
    43, 46

circulation clerks, 12
classification systems,
    23–24, 28
conservationists, 8, 29–30,
    31, 40, 51, 54
curators/curating, 48–49
cyberlibrarians, 8, 55

D
Dewey decimal system,
    24, 28

E
ephemera, 40
Eratosthenes, 20–21

F
finding aids, 42

G
genealogy, researching, 49
Gutenberg, Johannes,
    22–23
Gutenberg Bible, 23, 25, 51

About the Author

Laura Leone has an M.F.A in creative writing, and a master in library and information science (M.L.S.). She has worked as a psychiatric counselor, a freelance writer, a mathematics editor, and presently works as a book cataloger. She is always in the middle of at least one book. Originally from New York, she lives in Boston.

Photo Credits

Cover, pp. 21, 22, 25, 34 © Super Stock; pp. 2, 15, 39, 41 © Corbis; pp. 7, 9, 13, 18, 44, 50 © Cindy Reiman; pp. 16, 29, 32, 37, 43, 52 © The Image Works; pp. 47, 54 © Associated Press.

Design

Nelson Sá